A LESSON IN
NARRATIVE TIME

A LESSON IN NARRATIVE TIME

POEMS BY Jody Bolz

*For Ruth and Mark,
with affection —
and with hope for
poetry*

Jody

November 21, 2004

GIHON BOOKS

JOHNSON · VERMONT

2004

Publication of this volume is made possible in part by Z-ARTS (ZURICH-PARIS), Zelda Sherbourne Petté, and generous support from The Vermont Studio Center, Perspectives Fund, Harp Foundation, and the counsel of The Stinehour Press. To these, along with Delia Meisalis, Michael Ford and Michelle Favorsall, we owe our heartfelt thanks.

Published by Gihon Books
P.O. Box 613B
Johnson, Vermont 05656
Published in the United States of America

ISBN: 0-9761347-0-5

First Gihon Printing, 2004

Grateful acknowledgement is made to the following publications, in which portions of *A Lesson in Narrative Time*, sometimes in slightly different forms, first appeared: *The American Scholar* for section I of "Lessons in Narrative Time"; *Gargoyle* for "Ambush"; *The G.W. Review* for "Darling"; *Ploughshares* for "Last Draft of the Day's Light"; *Autumn Harvest* (Oxford Prize anthology, 2001, John Morgan, ed.) for section III of "Lessons in Narrative Time."

Many thanks to the Rona Jaffe Foundation for its support, to Jane Shore for her careful attention to this book as it took shape, and to Maxine Clair, Karen Sagstetter, Tony Hoagland, David McAleavey, Jane Vandenburgh, Samantha Guerry, and Carol Beehler.

Cover design: Carol Beehler & Paul Hoffmann
Cover photograph: Roy Gumpel/Getty Images

Designed and printed at The Stinehour Press
Lunenburg, Vermont

CONTENTS

Prelude
9

Ambush
13

Darling
19

Lessons in Narrative Time
27

Leroy Among the Starlings
35

Soundtrack
41

Prank Calls
47

Last Draft of the Day's Light
55

Day Apart
59

nothing though, not stone
nor light lasts
like the place I keep
the love of you in and this

though nothing can write it down
and nothing keep it:
nothingness
lasts long enough to keep it.

—A. R. AMMONS

FOR MY FAMILY

PRELUDE

You know it alters everything
    to be this scared
        that your heart's failing—
        cracked lens of your senses
        scattered in a swoon
I give it up
    I give up
        such uncanny willingness

        or loss of will
    makes fainting almost sexual
the body insisting
    and no will to resist
        the greying out
        a black tumbling pitch
        into nothing
then the full-body throbbing

        that's brought you back so far
            pulse slamming in your palate
        your tongue   your neck
    your temples
each limb trembles
    icy but restored
        the cool sweat sweet
        on your waking face

and you feel strangely grateful
to have an affliction that exalts
what you used to think
was common   was given
that exalts what you thought
was no miracle   just living:
joy's closest
close to vanishing

a scene you understand
just before it ends
and the room reels
with longing
this is what I wanted
this is what I want
as if later you could summon it
reassembling midnight   May

your husband beside you
in shadows and secrecy
a scuffle at the window
sudden rain   then lightning
that dazzles the magnolia leaves
bedroom bright   and brightening
a tableau fixed forever
in the moment it's over.

I. AMBUSH

AMBUSH

The drive to work isn't
the same drive every day:
new notes climb the clef
(open chord of dailiness)
and as to chance

as to whose car follows yours
or whose yours follows
how today's light
angles through the window-glass
today's sky transfigures

the river and the monuments
what in your experience
prepares you for this moment
when you recognize
(one hand on the steering wheel

one foot on the brake)
think you recognize
the driver stalled
in traffic just ahead
as he turns to watch

sculls racing past Key Bridge
the profile *his* profile
long jaw set as if
he's whistling to
the Irish aire

you're listening to
impossible to tell
even when his eyes lift
and a swatch of face
brow to cheekbones

fills the rearview mirror
of his red station wagon
he's watching you watching him
ambush   motors idling
your own face

a bad cartoon
framed by the windshield
"ex-wife"   "stranger"
and in the second's stillness
he doesn't react

even when the traffic starts
then shifts into first
a beat behind
accelerates   bearing right
the very direction

he'd take if he were driving
that car with Virginia plates
the very car he'd drive
if he were driving
a man with a family now

but if it isn't he
why lay your old love's mask
across the thrum and blur
the rush hour
mimicking some metaphor

that breaks
the chord of dailiness
making you forget
forsaking all others
forcing you backwards

to rock ledge   sage scrub
Alcova in September
more than 20 years ago
to search with him
for arrowheads a week

after his mother's death
her ashes scattered   *Penny*
where scouring through rubble
squatting in the open
you turn to say

"This could be—"
to no one
since he's vanished
in the interval
no answer to your whistle

so you shout his name
you shout for him
the second's stillness warning
faultline   seizure
you stop dead

you spin and squint
ransacking the visible
when he rises
from a creekbed
holding out an arrowhead

"What's wrong?"
estrangement frames him
flute trill   fade-out
world news on the radio
Baghdad   cloning   Kosovo

you drift
into the parking lot
switch off the ignition—
car key cold as agate in
the hollow of your hand.

II. DARLING

DARLING

She knows it's an act
when Taz waves
beneath the awning
of his whirring sidewalk cart
shouts "Darling–"
asking what she'll have
("Good morning, darling")
but she smiles

without wariness
he smiles back
she likes his Belgian accent
his tidy cart
the coffee menu's
cheerful pastel swirls
and exclamation points
likes the hopeful still-life

of commerce on his counter
shining spoons and creamers
cocoa shakers   cinnamon
she likes him
winces at the drag
of his injured right hand
(a motorcycle accident)
tamping the expresso press

and laughs at his banter:
"You Americans pay 40 million
to trash Clinton when you could get
the dirt on me for 40 bucks!"
he smiles glibly   handing down a cup
as she hands up the money
takes a napkin   thanks him
leans into the workday

to the music of moving
familiar office waiting
plum trees blowing
in a filmy square of sun
one searing sip of coffee
through the lid's sharp opening
two students smoking
outside the heavy door

she pushes with her hip
glass cold through cotton slacks
toward a carnival of voices
the clamor between classes
mail cart   ATM machine
then sprints for the elevator
following a janitor
coiled in extension cords

three students hauling backpacks
("The fourth question was bullshit—
we never even talked
about the troubadour poets!")
aftershave and coffee
briefcase against belly   *Five*
purse under her arm
"Would you press six?"

doors part on her corridor
the stink of blueprint toner
from the engineering office
just around the corner
floor-to-ceiling windows
featuring Washington in spring
so bright she blinks
as she passes

pulling keys from her pocket
turns the lock on her office
sunlight rifling bookshelves
desk a pageant of photographs
Brad   Molly   Eli   Jess
she drops her bags
switches on the radio
(a Bach cello concerto)

settles in to shuffle through
a stack of student stories
before stopping to see Faye
whose door's already open
at the far end of the hall
and soon they'll all be here
Janie   Maxine   David
Pati   Judith   Vik

but now the building's quiet
as she fixes on a picture
a photo from her honeymoon
holds it in both hands
and studies it   frowning
her husband at dusk
on the blue wall of a ruin
Sri Lanka in April

the very same person
who left her bed this morning
the one who reenchants her
after silences and screaming
familiar rasp of evening
scrapping with the children
after cooking and cleaning
reading   bathing   sleeping

the hundred gestures
of love and inattention
the transporting rise to sex
blind dancing   starlit
after false alarms   winter walks
bone-deep disappointment
after fire   fever   nightmare
at the graves of their fathers

after insult   rapture
harvest moon   willow branch
flutes and drums and welcome home
the arm's-length dispiriting
of age's slow clear changes
sometimes a stranger
"What's wrong?" she asks him
and he answers with a question

"Can't I even think alone?"
sometimes a lover
who pulls her by the hips
to the edge of their mattress
pins her hands with his
looks right at her
as if this joy were new to them
as if she'll never lose him.

III. LESSONS IN NARRATIVE TIME

LESSONS IN NARRATIVE TIME

I.

Sell your cleverness and buy bewilderment.
—RUMI

In the empty classroom
    you call roll without speaking
    and the missing stir in vacant chairs
(here—still here)
    until the heavy door shifts

and students jam the entrance
    students who are always young
    nineteen   twenty   twenty-one
though you're consigned to aging.
    What a weird arrangement—

Aaron   Leah   Dave
    in place of Adam   Sarah   Robb.
    You smile as you greet them
glancing at your notebook:
    Back-story and pacing

(see page 80—"Signs and Symbols").
    Drizzle dulls the window.
    Maryam   Jacob   Azza
for April   Jon   Roberto
    an imperfect equation

that makes change its constant.
    Watching their pens drift
  across each blue-lined page
you hear yourself explain
    how stories are assembled

from summary and scene.
    Valentina (late again)
  enters smiling vaguely
slides in next to Jacob
    at the far end of the table

long neck blotchy with arousal
    or embarrassment—
  she's bolted from a lover's bed
and run to school this once
    without the cultured

indifference   that thoroughbred
    loveliness with which she's kept
  her distance. . . .
Some mystery is essential
    but suspense is not enough.

Her father could be a spy
    instead of a diplomat
  (they've lived in eastern Europe).
Conflict's not enough unless
    it tugs a thread of revelation.

Jacob's eyes rivet now
      on Valentina's hand
   which flies
to pull a rubber band
     from musky sun-streaked hair.

Tension is essential
      in a pattern of change
   but structure's secondary.
So fuck
    the Freitag triangle—

this is not geometry—
      and toss easy reverie
   in slo-mo fade-outs
and flashbacks of eager sex.
    Passion's not enough

in fiction.
     Craft is not enough
   and edge is not enough.
Confession's not enough.
    So fuck nonfiction

parading as fiction
    and fuck fiction
   posing as fact.
Voyeurism's not enough.
    Did Jacob get his tongue

pierced first
or after Valentina?
See what's happened
to the oral tradition . . .
when either speaks

a gold stud gleams:
O bright revelation!
Plot's a fine contrivance
gears and flywheels
shimmering—

The rain stops.
A truck honks.
Leah takes
her glasses off.
Valentina's hand goes up.

II.

Beauty pricked her finger
and the kingdom lost a century

harp strings moldering beside an open hand
through a hundred songless summers

until love scaled the vine-choked gate
to rouse time with a kiss:

the curse was never death
but dreaming agelessness.

III.

If nothing lasts
make your subject nothing
the nothing you'll recover
and the nothing you'll restore

make nothing your ambition
invisible or blinding
dear friends at your table
fire   woodwinds   laughter

sleighbells knock an opening door
and children barrel in
the lacework of each bootprint
unravelling as you watch it.

IV. LEROY AMONG THE STARLINGS

LEROY AMONG THE STARLINGS

Redemption soars from Leroy's gate-house
weekdays after three when he starts
his shift at the parking lot
and she ends hers   attending what?
"Hey dear, you're in 8"
he ambles from the pegboard
holding out her key
rakish smile   southern lilt

cool-cat gait more FM jazz
than AM gospel   but it's gospel
he's listening to   divine exhortations
issued across asphalt
by a grubby transistor
workdays after three when he starts
his shift at the parking lot
and she heads home

from nothing clear as his routine
Lord guide us on our journey
out of Leroy's tabernacle
(wafting smoke-and-sandwich staleness)
past lanky agile Leroy
keeper of the keys
a uniformed black Methodist
vigorous at 66 despite the stroke

that left his limp
and never sanctimonious
no   he's freely sardonic
on the delicate subject
of gating this college lot
(brand-new yellow scanners
poised to read IDs)
"Never when . . ." he tells her

in reply to a question
about gate activation
"Don't let appearance fool you"
but she does   or she did
take last Thursday
how she left work late
walking here at sunset
and was stunned to find him

tossing bread on gravel
while starlings swooped and grovelled
'Why are you amazed,' the angel asked
never to have guessed
that Leroy enjoys feeding birds?
The guy could be Saint Francis
and she'd never even notice
in her Jewish insularity

her gated affability
"You usually gone before 11's free"
Eleven?   "They won't eat
but in that one space—see?"
she saw it now   of course she did
as she tracked hopping starlings
tseeeer   tseeeer   tseeeer   whooee
bun crumbs in their golden beaks

parading iridescent wings
in parking space 11
Sing praises to His name children
praise the Bread of Heaven
until Leroy in dusty blue
returned from the car-lot booth
familiar and a mystery
with the key to her Odyssey.

V. SOUNDTRACK

SOUNDTRACK

Despite banality
and mindful of it
despite dirty floors
breakfast plates
leaf blight   lost bearings

you rush in at four
on a bleat   a furrowed G
Jake's voice   "Check your reed?"
the skittering of fingers
"Tighten up the screw, Jess"

bungled prelude
to your daughter's music lesson
and lean into the living room
she smiles   lifts her saxophone
lipping the mouthpiece

as Jake starts on the piano
an unfamiliar intro
and you step out of your work shoes
into the kitchen
to pour a glass of water

grateful to be home
despite lost lists   missed cues
set against a background
of confusion and retreat
but the first clear measure

stops you mid-gesture
      staring at windowplants
(jasmine   cymbidium)
  until they blur and swagger
     while you stand there

                          glass in hand
                 mouthing words your parents sang
                      Time after time . . .
                  (then something something) *I'm*
          so lucky . . .

  it's true
     despite routine's
circling wonderlessness
  belly pressed to counter-edge
     head back   drinking fast

                     lucky to be
               the one you run to see . . .
                    "Slow it down now—slower, Jess"
               Jake's broken piano chords progress
            behind the bolting melody

  "Tongue OFF the beat
     not ON, okay?"
love's conscious exultation
  over now   your home itself
    the proving ground

shadow of a family
swaying on the wall each
            sabbath   birthday   *yahrzeit*
the children's faces floating
eerily in the half-light

though you admit to loneliness
    admit that love confounds you
your *family* confounds you—
  Jessie hits a flat   corrects
    waiting out the piano phrase

                and time after time
        within the blinding intimate
                (son sprawled on his lamplit bed
            incense smoke   sports radio
        daughter at the mirror

    fastening a gold barrette
        each room a diorama
of guttering innocence
  husband in the hallway
    with his arms full of laundry)

                you hear the blue note argue
        an ardor beyond aging:
                first you were lovers—
            and *this*
        the dreaming future.

VI. PRANK CALLS

PRANK CALLS

"Arroz by any other name . . ."
you quip across the simmering rice

grinning at your 12-year-old
all jiggle and grimace

slouched over an atlas
hissing

"Stop it, Mom
you know I hate geography—

you'll make me lose the Pyrenees,
and this retainer's killing me."

Jessie tugs the wire
frowning at the south of France.

Rumble on the big front porch
and suddenly you're in the comics:

THWACK!AND!THUNDER!
BOYS!ON!BLADES!

Jess says   "Great—Eli's home.
Now nobody can concentrate."

The blue door bangs
against the wall.

"Skates off"   you yell
"or stay outside!"

Muffled protests
thuds and knocks

four teenaged boys
in rank white socks.

Your firstborn
sidles past the stove

prospecting for ice
four glasses and a tray

pours lemonade   (his own
Gerard's   Cooper's   Ben's).

Jessie blinks
and caps her pen.

"I don't see why we have to learn
a zillion names of rivers.

What use is it in later life?"
indicating *later life*

is what she sees you living.
"You'll go to Europe someday, Jess."

She sneers   then mugs
an earnest glance.

"Oh, Pierre—is that the Loire?
I learned of it in middle school!"

She shimmies off the kitchen stool
lugs her textbooks to the hall.

"I'll be at Anne-Marie's, okay?
You can call me when they're gone."

Eli snags the cordless phone
"Where's the DC phone book, Mom?"

You point to the cupboard
which he opens for the white pages

swaggers to the living room
carrying the tattered book

and all the boys pore over it
like baby-faced degenerates . . .

Ben emits a wicked laugh
"Stop right there.

That's perfect, guys—
Arlene Slutt on Wilson Lane!

Or is Arlene a geezer name?
Wait, let me try again.

Whoa—that's it:
Abdul Dicko, 724-2185!"

Gerard bristles   "He'll think
we're anti-Arab, man."

Cooper swarms the crowded couch—
"Move over while I find a WASP. . . .

Hey, Richard Head's an Anglo name."
Eli coughs and skulks away.

"E-man—don't be a wuss.
You said before you'd go first!"

Eli's *out* is sweet Ms. Slutt
"I'll go next, Coop. Dick's your hit."

Cooper takes the telephone
presses in the *traceless* code

then the number
"Hope he's home—"

What if Dick Head's sick or sad
unemployed and impotent?

The phone book must be
two years old—

"Hello, ma'm.
Is Richard there?"

Jesus—is it Mrs. Head?
A widow now if Dick's dead!

"Mr. Head? This is Dean
from Tyler Systems, Inc.

May I call you Di—
Damn it, he hung up on me!"

Cooper really looks surprised.
"Let me try—"   Eli's back

"I'm dying to ask Arlene out!"
How many jerks have phoned Ms. Slutt?

"Don't hang up if she sounds old."
E frowns at Ben and takes the phone.

"Good afternoon, is Arlene home?
Oh—hello.   I'm calling

with a quick request.
No—   No, I don't think we've met.

This is just a courtesy call—
I don't think so.   Not tonight—

I'm calling just—   I beg your pardon?
What?   A prank?

If you don't wish to take my call
please put on another Slutt."

Gerard's in spasms on the rug.
Cooper cackles   "That's enough."

Why didn't you nip this in the bud?
When Eli's off you nab the phone.

"Out, thugs . . .
or I'll call the cops."

They're stumbling across the porch—
grabbing goals and skates and pucks

the din receding
WHOOSH!AND!GONE!

It's six o'clock:
the news is on.

VII. LAST DRAFT OF THE DAY'S LIGHT

LAST DRAFT OF THE DAY'S LIGHT

Not wilderness exactly
open country
a wooded valley
and the river in it
waterfall and towpath

footbridge   lockhouse
a canal that runs to Cumberland
beside the Potomac   not
wilderness   you know that
bounded parkland

with your neighborhood above it
stage set by some Luminist
where you describe
the hour   convinced
no calendar can register

a day's encounters
no photograph expose
love's figure in the garden
no map locate
the river you'll remember

as glint and roar at floodstage
under sycamore branches
the puzzle-patterned bark ablaze
fragments of a torn page
suspended now   brightening

a last draft
of the day's light
tossed away   then salvaged
the reassembled story
of a run by the river

with your friend beside you
talking as you listen   Jane
describing the contents
of her dead aunt's
hope chest

"lace-work, mirror, dresser set
and every card we ever sent"
the drumming
at your temples
when you turn and see

two shadows
cross the cutbank   "Look—"
quick ciphers on a golden scrim:
the future-haunted present
racing on.

VIII. DAY APART

DAY APART

My little brother died. . . . My mother some days later found
his footprint in the yard and tried to build something
over it to keep the wind from blowing it away.
                                    —A. R. AMMONS

You take the day apart
and reassemble it
forget the clock
forget the family heading back

and take what's gone apart
to reassemble it:
gates open on a farmyard
blown dust   woman kneeling

tricking up a shelter
with rubble and short sticks
over the footprint of a child
her own son three days dead

as if her will to foil time
could take the grief apart
the simple fact
of *her* deliberateness

your own starting point
bland spring sunlight
angling to dusk above the house
where you're sitting

a mother yourself
bent over her story
trying to make sense
of this one day in particular

waking in the half-dark
your husband already up
cat-cry   shower spilling
at the end of the narrow hall

world news on the radio
this day and no other day
in any other life
turn it in the light

sweet transformation
blue flame blossoming
your quick hand
combing back your hair

as you wait by the stove
a woman in a nightdress
and a worn white robe
here in the home

where you live with your family
these rooms where you're loved
and sometimes hated
bright table by the windows

for your son and your daughter
who come downstairs and sit
eat their toast
read the comics

rangy adolescents
they shoulder their backpacks
amble out
"Goodbye" from the porch

the schoolbus glides into view
its strict doors opening . . .
you go back in
sit down among the empty cups

take *common* apart
see in dailiness
a great improvisation
with everything at stake

its motives shared or private
each entrance and each exit
the gestures   speeches   warnings
soliloquies and conflicts

love scenes   reveries
each unscripted act
forming on its own
and if you take one scene apart

to reassemble it
you lose surprise
the thrown book   the weeping
you're sorry   so sorry

how you wish you could
set it right
wish you could stop worrying
feverish at two a.m.

trapped in dread
your heart's dead beat
stalling and striking ("sudden
death" the doctor said)

but here you are again
at dawn
here   still here
waking in the half-dark

your husband already out
you reach for a robe
shuffle into slippers
raise the blind on your yard

expecting the hazy lawn
a bicycle   your neighbor's
cottage garden but
see instead

the dry ground
of a dirt farm
woman in a house-dress
bending down to gather sticks

shadows conspiring
with her fingers in the dust
as you dream yourself
standing a story above her

right palm
pressing window-glass
left hand heavy
on the nape of your neck

seeing wet grass
a bicycle   your neighbor's
cottage garden but
you're late

you have to hurry
they'll need breakfast
bag lunches
wash up and go downstairs

the coffee's warm
newpaper's in
put the kettle on for tea
bread in the toaster

pour the juice
before they're downstairs
in the hall
scrambling for shoes

on the floor by the mirror
where a dark-eyed woman
squints into the glare
above the heads of her children

quick hands tying back
her wild hair
(is that white at the temples?
is she shamming a smile?)

turns away to kettle-whistle
sugar   butter   lunch bags
for her son and her daughter
who eat and read

until their friends
come through the door
Gerard   Dan   Patrick
Sara   Anne-Marie

"The bus—"
goodbye from the porch
you go back in
sit down among the empty cups

take *empty* apart
beginning with what's missing
name the dead
and count them

remembering the wide world
as it was when you began
Gus   Etta   Tillie
Dora   Frances   Mary

constellations dimmed
and disappearing
Max   Betty   Stewart
Sanford   Cyril   Ruth

leaving you one uncle now
one aunt
half your cousins
strangers in homes

you'll never see
and just this year
your mother-in-law
your brother-in-law

add them to the list
you're working on
Margy   Brad   Charlie
David   Penny   George

then count the living
dead to you
the lover you won't see again
waking in his own home

lake-water   buoy bell
memory a rumor
at the edges of his bed
missing   yes

but you've forgotten
to get dressed
so climb the steps
one foot   then the other

gaze at the laundry
on the bench by the bed
as your vision
silvers out and you slump

cross-legged to the floor
blank page in a book of hours
white field darkening
as a list begins to form

David   Penny   George
Jane   Ron
with a new name at the end
blurred but legible

a new name
in your own strong script . . .
ridiculous—
in seconds you can stand

breathing slowly
counting breaths
leaning on the doorjamb
ready now

to take the room apart
and reassemble it
a stumbling heartbeat
holding you in place:

Exhibit A at the museum
of lost chances
poised between the doorway
and the nightstand

as your eyes scan
laundry   bookshelves
red birds flaring
from the *huipil* on the wall

bright-beaded moccasin
candle in a cup
your husband's glasses
shining on an open book

and at the window
hanging from its string
a palm-sized crystal
that takes the light apart

and reassembles it
the white walls antic
wheeling rainbow flames
and even now

you find it beautiful
a beauty without resonance
you know you could be happy here
you know you *have* been happy

how many nights
in the dreaming dark
how many mornings
skin on skin

your husband's warm hand
smoothing back your hair
the history of this single room
another kind of light

and your task to divide it
blown dust   seconds passing
quick fingers pressing on a pen
believing it's the charge of love

to shelter   to enshrine
but what are
rubble   sticks   words
love itself   faced with

now and now and now
one minute   then another
the line extends
breaks off

and starts again
stubborn   deliberate
a hopeful act
as if your will to foil time

could take the truth apart
and reassemble it
set it down
set it right forever

hopeful or naive
or hopeful *and* naive
eager still   but eager
for what time   what place

the last light on whose face
in what clearing
wild iris   stream-sounds
the coming dark

simply night
a beauty without resonance
constellations
brightening to blaze

and you too young
to view your life
with anything like tenderness
untested   unbetrayed

the now and now a dance for you
when minutes passed
like wheeling rainbow flames
and offered chances

gate flung on a garden
gate flung on a city street
the wide world spreading out
bright pages in a book of hours

revelation   work   desire
seasons reeled   a star show
one year
then another

two decades gone
then three
bringing you this moment
in this bedroom

making you this figure
on this threshold
poised between your dreamlife
and the workday

old enough
to view the scene
with something like nostalgia
blindsided by tenderness

sickening on failure
stubborn and deliberate
a mother folding laundry
and putting it away.

NOTE:

The A. R. Ammons quote on page 59 is drawn from an interview by William Walsh, first published in Michigan Quarterly Review *(Winter 1989). The full paragraph reads:*

"The most powerful image of my emotional life is something I had repressed and one of my sisters lately reminded me of. It was when my little brother, who was two and a half years younger than I, died at eighteen months. My mother some days later found his footprint in the yard and tried to build something over it to keep the wind from blowing it away. That is the most powerful image I've ever known."